D1104012

Hydrogen

THE PERIODIC TABLE

Nigel Saunders

Heinemann Library
Chicago, Illinois

Customer Service 888-454-2279

Visit our website at www.heinemannlibrary.com

Design: Ian Winton
Illustrations: Stefan Chabluk
Picture Research: Vashti Gwynn
Originated by Ambassador Litho Ltd.
Printed and bound in China by
South China Printing Company

Produced for Heinemann by Discovery Books Ltd.

08 07 06 05 04
10 9 8 7 6 5 4 3 2 1

**Library of Congress
Cataloging-in-Publication Data**
Saunders, N. (Nigel)
  Hydrogen / Nigel Saunders.
      v. cm. -- (The periodic table)
Includes bibliographical references and index.
Contents: Elements and atomic structure -- The periodic table and hydrogen -- Hydrogen right from the start -- Inflammable air -- Hydrogen oxide -- Corrosive hydrogen -- Hydrogen in complex molecules -- Here comes the sun -- Find out more.
  ISBN 1-4034-1663-X (HC), 1-4034-5497-3 (Pbk.)
  1. Hydrogen--Juvenile literature. [1. Hydrogen. 2. Chemical
elements.] I. Title. II. Series.
  QD181.H1S19 2003
                        553.92--dc21

Acknowledgments
The author and publishers are grateful to the following for permission to reproduce copyright material: p. 4 George Lepp/Corbis; p. 8 Michael Dunning/Science Photo Library; pp. 11, 12, 22, 24, 55(bottom) NASA; pp. 13, 47 Adam Hart-Davis/Science Photo Library; p. 15 bottom Physics Department, Imperial College/Science Photo Library; pp. 15 top, 17 Bettmann/Corbis; p. 16 Hulton-Deutsch Collection/Corbis; p. 18 Kevin Fleming/Corbis; p. 19 Volker Steger/Science Photo Library; p. 20 Philip Gould/Corbis; pp. 23, 43 top Ralph A. Clevenger/Corbis; p. 26 RNT Productions/Corbis; p. 27 Caroline Penn/Corbis; pp. 28, 33, 41 Charles D. Winters/Science Photo Library; p. 29 Martin Bond/ Science Photo Library; p. 30 Ray Juno/Corbis; pp. 34, 35 Andrew Lambert Photography/Science Photo Library; p. 38 Ted Spiegel/ Corbis; p. 43 bottom Tecmap Corporation; p. 45 Tom Stewart Photography/Corbis; p. 48 Pascal Goetgheluck/ Science Photo Library; p. 49 Astrid & Hans Frieder Michler/Science Photo Library; p. 50 Dr. Tim Evans/Science Photo Library; p. 51 Richard T. Nowitz/Corbis; p. 53 Thorn Lang/Corbis; p. 55 (top) David Frazier/Science Photo Library; p. 56 Thom Lang/Corbis.
Cover photograph of a water droplet, reproduced with permission of Corbis.

The author would like to thank Angela, Kathryn, David and Jean for all their help and support. Special thanks to Theodore Dolter for his review of this book.

Contents

CHAPTER 1

Elements and Atomic Structure

Everything is made from chemicals, even you. Most chemicals are solids. However, some are gases, like the air, and others are liquids, like water. Some chemicals are very big and complex, such as the proteins that make up your skin and hair, while others are simpler, like the oxygen you need to stay alive. There are millions of different chemicals, which can be solid, liquid, or gas, or complex or simple. But they are all made from a few very basic substances called elements.

This is the start of a balloon race. Everything you can see here, including the balloons, vehicles, and the people, is made from some of the millions of substances in the world. Some of the substances, like the oxygen in the hot air filling the balloons, will be elements but most will be compounds.

Elements and compounds

Elements are chemicals that cannot be broken down into simpler ones using chemical reactions. There are about ninety elements that occur naturally, and scientists have learned how to make over twenty more using nuclear reactions. Most elements are metals, such as iron and magnesium, but some are nonmetals, such as carbon and oxygen. Elements can join together in chemical reactions to make compounds. For instance, iron reacts with oxygen to make iron oxide, while carbon reacts with oxygen to form carbon dioxide. Most of the different chemicals in the world are compounds, made up of two or more elements chemically joined together.

Atoms

All chemicals are made up of tiny particles called atoms. Elements contain atoms that are all the same, while compounds are made from two or more types of atoms joined together. Although you can see most of the chemicals around you, individual atoms are too tiny to see, even with a microscope. Hydrogen is the simplest and smallest atom of all. It is about two and a half billion times smaller than a soccer ball.

Subatomic particles

Atoms are incredibly tiny, but they are made from even smaller objects called subatomic particles. At the center of each atom is a nucleus. It contains the biggest subatomic particles, which are protons and neutrons. Arranged around the nucleus are even smaller subatomic particles called electrons. Subatomic particles are so small that most of an atom is just empty space.

electron

nucleus of
one proton

This is a model of an atom of hydrogen. The nucleus of each hydrogen atom usually contains one proton, although sometimes there are one or two neutrons as well. An electron is arranged in a shell, or energy level, around it.

Groups

Elements react with one another in different ways, which makes chemistry very exciting. However, working out all the reactions between the elements was difficult, so several people tried to organize the elements to make the work easier. A Russian chemist named Dimitri Mendeleev made the best attempt. In 1869 he made a table with eight groups, putting similar elements into each group. Chemists found they could predict what would happen when they carried out chemical reactions. Mendeleev's table was so successful that it has evolved into the periodic table used today.

CHAPTER 2

The Periodic Table and Hydrogen

Chemists built on Mendeleev's work and produced the modern periodic table. Each row in the table is called a period. The elements in a period are arranged in order of increasing atomic number (number of protons in the nucleus). The columns in the table are called groups and there are eighteen. All the elements in each group have similar chemical properties. It is called the periodic table because these different chemical properties occur regularly or periodically.

An element's properties are decided by the way its electrons are positioned around the nucleus. Electrons are arranged in shells, like layers of an onion. Each element in a group has the same number of electrons in the shell furthest from the nucleus, called the outer shell. For example all the elements in group 1 are very reactive metals and have one electron in their outer shells. The group 7 elements are very reactive and have seven electrons in their outer shells.

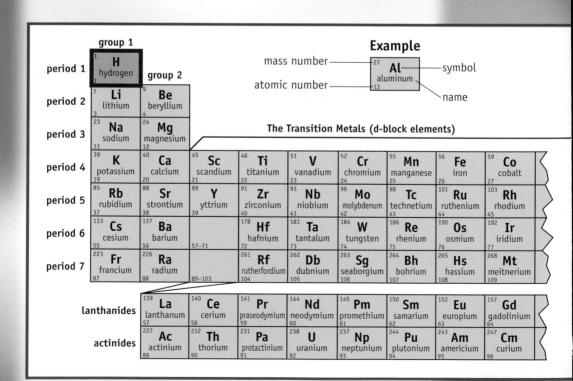

The properties of the elements change gradually as you go down a group. For example, the elements in group 17 become less reactive and their melting points increase. At the top of the group, fluorine and chlorine are both gases at room temperature. Fluorine is the most reactive element of all, even reacting with glass. Bromine, in the middle of the group, is the only nonmetal element that is liquid at room temperature. Near the bottom of the group, iodine is solid at room temperature and is far less reactive than the three elements above it.

Hydrogen

Hydrogen only has one electron and this periodic table shows it above lithium in group 1, but hydrogen does not belong there at all because it has such different properties. In some periodic tables hydrogen is shown by itself. Hydrogen is a very special element and has many uses, as you will discover in this book.

▼ *This is the periodic table of the elements. Although hydrogen is often shown at the top of group 1, it does not belong to the group because it is a nonmetal and is very different from the metallic elements in group 1.*

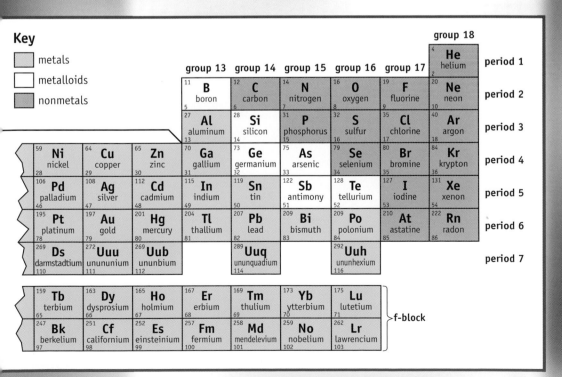

CHAPTER 3

Hydrogen Right from the Start

Nobody was around when the universe began, so it is difficult to be certain what happened. However, scientists have gathered evidence about the universe. They have used this evidence to describe how they think the universe started. Their theory is called the Big Bang, and it seems that hydrogen was there almost from the very beginning.

Too hot to handle

The universe started as something incredibly tiny and hot around 15 billion years ago. In the Big Bang, there was a massive explosion and the universe expanded very quickly and began to cool down. The temperature of the universe at this time was more than you can imagine. A Bunsen burner can heat up to about 1,000 °C (1,800 °F). But about a hundredth of a second after the Big Bang, the temperature of the universe was about 100,000,000,000 °C (180,000,000,000 °F)! All sorts of tiny particles appeared and disappeared in a fiery soup that was full of energy and radiation. Protons and neutrons formed as the universe continued to cool, but it was still too hot for them to stick together to make the nuclei of atoms.

Protons and neutrons

Protons and neutrons are even smaller than atoms and sometimes lighter. A proton is so light that one septillion of them would only have a mass of one gram! Obviously this makes it very difficult to discuss their masses sensibly. Because protons and neutrons are almost identical in mass, you can use a relative scale to compare their masses more easily. For example, if the mass of a proton is 1, the mass of a neutron is also 1.

From nothing to three nuclei in three minutes!

Scientists believe the universe kept on cooling very quickly after the Big Bang, and after about three minutes it had cooled to about 1,000,000,000 °C (1,800,000,000 °F). This was cold enough for protons and neutrons to stick together to make the nuclei of atoms. Over 90 percent of the nuclei were hydrogen nuclei, made from just one proton or a proton with one or two neutrons stuck on. The rest were mostly helium nuclei, each made from two protons and two neutrons stuck together. There were also a few lithium nuclei, each made from three protons and four neutrons.

Electrons were also whizzing around the universe. But before they could slow down enough to stay with the nuclei to form atoms, the universe had to cool down even more.

◀ This artwork shows how scientists think the Big Bang looked. Scientists believe that the universe began as something incredibly tiny and exploded outwards about 15 billion years ago. Hydrogen, helium, and lithium atoms were the first atoms formed as the universe became bigger and cooler.

Atoms Everywhere!

Hundreds of thousands of years passed before the universe cooled down enough for the first electrons to stay with the nuclei to make atoms. However, when they did, about three-quarters of the atoms were hydrogen.

Attractive electrons

Neutrons have no electrical charge, but protons are positively charged. Electrons are negatively charged, so they are strongly attracted to the positive protons in a nucleus. But electrons only began to stay with nuclei when the universe had cooled to 3,000 °C (5,400 °F). Once this happened, atoms started to form. About a million years after the Big Bang, all the nuclei had joined with electrons to form atoms.

The three subatomic particles

This are the properties of protons, neutrons and electrons.

particle	relative mass	relative charge	position in atoms
proton	1	+1	nucleus
neutron	1	0	nucleus
electron	$1/1836$	-1	shells

Electrons and protons have opposite charges. However, their electrical charges are the same size, even though electrons are nearly two thousand times lighter than protons.

Hydrogen in the universe

Most hydrogen atoms are made from just one proton with one electron arranged around it. However, some hydrogen atoms also contain one or two neutrons. Atoms that have the same number of protons and electrons, but different numbers of neutrons are called isotopes.

This is the center of the Orion nebula, seen through the Hubble ▶
Space Telescope. Hundreds of new stars are forming inside the
nebula's gigantic swirling mass of gas and dust.

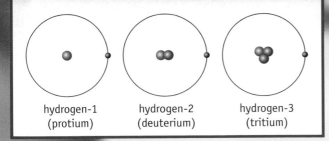

hydrogen-1
(protium)

hydrogen-2
(deuterium)

hydrogen-3
(tritium)

▲
These are models of the three hydrogen isotopes. Each atom contains just one proton and one electron, but the nucleus of hydrogen-2 also has a neutron and the nucleus of hydrogen-3 contains two neutrons.

Most hydrogen isotopes are hydrogen-1 (protium) and have one proton but no neutrons in their nuclei. Atoms of hydrogen-2 (deuterium) have one proton and one neutron. Atoms of hydrogen-3 (tritium) have one proton and two neutrons. All three isotopes react the same way chemically because they have identical numbers of protons and electrons. However, they have different masses and some can be radioactive.

The first stars

Over millions of years, gravity gradually pulled atoms together to form big clumps. Really big clumps eventually formed stars. About two hundred million years after the Big Bang, the first stars lit up.

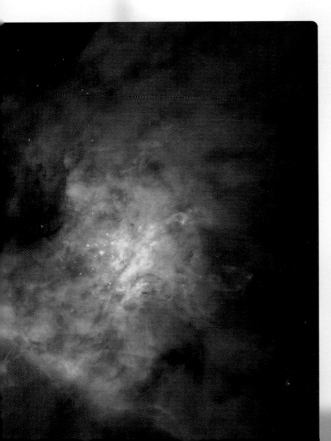

A star uses a type of nuclear reaction, called nuclear fusion, to produce its heated light. In a star, this involves hydrogen nuclei joining together to make helium nuclei and producing a tremendous amount of energy. Gravity pulls the star together and stops its exploding. However, as it gets older a star begins to run out of hydrogen and starts to shrink. Other nuclei join together and make the nuclei of new elements. Stars may shrink so fast that they explode, triggering a supernova. This causes material containing lots of elements to shoot out into space.

Star Dust

Planets in the solar system contain elements that come from the star dust produced by supernovae. The atoms in the food you eat, the air you breathe, and the water you drink—even you—come from this star dust.

The Milky Way

Galaxies are clusters of billions of stars. There may be over a hundred billion galaxies in the universe. The galaxy you live in is called the Milky Way. It contains over a hundred billion stars. But one star about two thirds of the way from the edge of the galaxy is very important because it is the Sun. Earth and the other planets in the solar system orbit round the Sun.

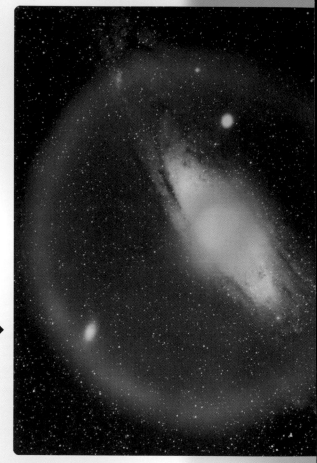

Galaxies come in many different shapes and sizes, including spinning disks like the Milky Way. The Milky Way contains the Sun and over a hundred billion other stars.

The solar system

The solar system began as a huge cloud of dust and gas in space, containing elements made in earlier stars. Gravity began to pull the cloud together and a spinning disk of material formed. The material in the cloud began to spiral inwards, a bit like the way that water spirals down a drain. It got hotter as it did this and eventually became so hot that nuclear reactions started. As a result, the Sun was formed about 5,000 million years ago. The planets formed about 4,600 million years ago from the remains of the cloud of dust and gas. The planets closest to the Sun (Mercury, Venus, Earth, and Mars) are rocky, whereas those farther away are made of gas. Earth is the only planet in the solar system to have large amounts of liquid water.

Where's all the hydrogen?

Hydrogen is the most abundant atom in the universe, in the Sun, and in seawater. It has the lightest atoms of all, which is why there are big differences between the two columns in the table below. Silicon and oxygen are the two most abundant elements in Earth's crust and together form 69 percent of its atoms.

This table shows the proportions of hydrogen in the universe, our Sun, Earth's crust, and seawater.

	Percent of atoms	Percent of mass
universe	93.0	76.0
the Sun	93.0	76.0
Earth's crust	3.1	0.1
seawater	66.2	10.7

Hydrogen on Earth

Hydrogen is only about the tenth most abundant atom in Earth's crust. Hydrogen atoms usually join together to make hydrogen molecules, H_2. Each hydrogen molecule contains two hydrogen atoms, joined together by a chemical bond. Earth's atmosphere contains very little hydrogen gas because it can easily escape into space. Luckily, most hydrogen atoms are joined with oxygen atoms to make water molecules. Each water molecule, H_2O, is made from two hydrogen atoms and one oxygen atom, joined together by chemical bonds.

▲ *Chemists often make models of molecules to help them explain the **reactions** they study. This is a model of a water molecule, H_2O. The white balls represent hydrogen atoms and the red ball represents an oxygen atom.*

CHAPTER 4

Inflammable Air

The properties of hydrogen

Hydrogen is a colorless gas. It has no odor and it is not poisonous. It does not dissolve very well in water. Only about 18 liters (19 quarts), or 1.5 grams (0.05 ounces), of hydrogen dissolves in a cubic meter (cubic yard) of water at room temperature. Hydrogen is a very reactive element; if a spark or flame is put into a mixture of hydrogen and air, the hydrogen reacts with the oxygen in the air and explodes.

The pop test for hydrogen

There is a simple laboratory test for hydrogen. The test relies on the reaction between hydrogen and oxygen in air. If a lighted piece of wood is put inside a test tube of hydrogen, the hydrogen burns very quickly and makes a popping sound. It can be really loud and squeaky if some air is let in first!

Hydrogen also explodes when mixed with very reactive gases, such as fluorine and chlorine. It reacts with hot metal oxides and removes the oxygen from them. These reactions form water, which is hydrogen oxide, leaving the metal behind.

The equation for copper oxide reacting with hydrogen is:

$$\text{copper oxide} + \text{hydrogen} \xrightarrow{\text{heat}} \text{copper} + \text{hydrogen oxide (water)}$$

$$CuO(s) + H_2(g) \xrightarrow{\text{heat}} Cu(s) + H_2O(l)$$

The discovery of hydrogen

Hydrogen is easily made by mixing metals and acids together, so hydrogen was actually discovered many times. However, most chemists did not realize that they had discovered a new element. They thought it was a type of air and was often called inflammable air. The word *inflammable* has the same meaning as *flammable,* which is "something that is easily set on fire."

In 1766 Henry Cavendish, an English chemist, finally discovered that inflammable air was really an element. In 1783 Antoine Lavoisier, a French chemist, discovered that water is the only substance made when inflammable air burns in air. Although Cavendish discovered hydrogen, it was Lavoisier who named it. The word *hydrogen* comes from the Greek words *hydro* and *genes,* meaning "water-forming."

◀ *The French chemist Antoine Lavoisier (1743–1794) discovered that hydrogen and oxygen react together to make water. Lavoisier (who is in the middle of this engraving) is seen showing other scientists one of his experiments on the different gases in air.*

Traces of hydrogen in sunlight

In 1862 Anders Ångström, a Swedish physicist, discovered hydrogen in the Sun by studying sunlight. The Sun produces light containing all the colors of the spectrum, although not all of them reach Earth. The hydrogen in the Sun absorbs some of the colors, leaving black lines in its spectrum. When hydrogen burns it produces its own spectrum. Ångström compared the missing colors in sunlight with the spectrum produced by hydrogen and realized that they matched exactly.

▼ *Scientists can work out which elements are in the Sun by studying its spectrum. Different elements absorb different colors in the spectrum, producing thousands of black lines. The line in the yellow part is caused by sodium.*

Into the Air with Hydrogen

Helium is often used to lift party balloons into the air because it has a low density. However, hydrogen has the lowest density of any of the elements. A liter (quart) of helium has a mass of 0.166 grams (0.006 ounces.), twice the mass of the same volume of hydrogen. This means that hydrogen should be even better than helium for lifting party balloons. However, there is a big problem with using hydrogen, as you will discover.

Getting balloons to go up

A liter of air weighs 1.2 grams (0.04 ounces.), while a liter of hydrogen weighs just 0.083 g (0.003 oz.)—more than one gram less! If the hydrogen's container weighed less than a gram, it would float up! Balloons are light enough to float when filled with hydrogen. Barrage balloons, which are enormous balloons filled with over 500 cubic meters (654 cubic yards) of hydrogen, were used in World War II to make it more difficult for enemy aircraft to fly over towns and cities. However, even these were tiny compared to the great airships.

Barrage balloons like these made things very difficult for enemy aircraft in World War II. They were 20 meters (22 yards) long and 9 meters (10 yards) high and were filled with hydrogen.

The *Hindenburg*

The *Hindenburg* was a huge airship designed by a German called Count von Zeppelin. It was 245 meters (268 yards) long, more than three times the length of a modern Boeing 747 airliner. The airship was kept in the air by 200,000 cubic meters (261,590 cubic yards) of hydrogen and could carry 50 crew members, 72 passengers and 11 tons of cargo. The *Hindenburg* went into service carrying passengers between Europe and the United States, but a terrible disaster awaited it at Lakehurs, New Jersey, in 1937.

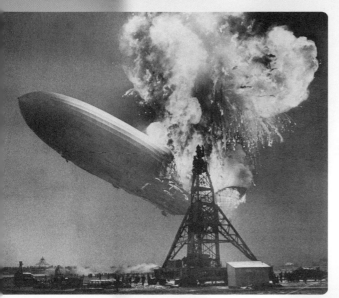

◄ *The* Hindenburg *was an enormous airship filled with hydrogen. While coming in to land on May 6, 1937, a spark caused by static electricity set its skin on fire. The hydrogen gas expanded and burst out of its containers, causing the* Hindenburg *to explode in a huge fireball.*

While trying to land at Lakehurst, the *Hindenburg* suddenly burst into flames. It was completely destroyed, killing many of the people on board. The huge amount of flammable hydrogen it was carrying was blamed for the explosion. After this accident and others, airships went out of fashion for a long time. Modern airships are much smaller and are lifted by helium rather than hydrogen. Unlike hydrogen, helium is not reactive and cannot ignite or explode.

Was hydrogen to blame?

Although hydrogen was blamed for starting the fire in the *Hindenburg*, aluminum may have been the problem. The *Hindenburg's* frame was covered with a fabric treated with a mixture of aluminum powder and iron oxide. This mixture is also called thermit and it is used to weld railway lines. When it catches fire, thermit reacts very strongly with huge flames, producing aluminum oxide and iron. It gets so hot that the iron melts!

Liquid Hydrogen

Hydrogen condenses to form a liquid at –253 °C (–459 °F). Liquid hydrogen is more than 60 times denser than hydrogen gas, so you can fit more of it into a container. This is useful if hydrogen is being used as a fuel, but the very low temperatures needed bring their own problems.

Cryogenics

The coldest temperature possible is –273.15 °C (–460 °F). This is called absolute zero. The temperature of liquid hydrogen is only 20 °C (68 °F) above this, so it really is incredibly cold. Ordinary refrigerators cannot reach temperatures like these, so special cryogenic refrigerators are needed. These machines require a lot of energy just to run. Many substances become brittle and break easily at these low temperatures, so special containers are needed to store and transport the liquid hydrogen. It might seem that liquid hydrogen is too tricky to use, but it is very useful for scientific research and powering rockets.

Bubble chambers

Subatomic particles such as protons, neutrons, and electrons are far too small to see. There are also other subatomic particles that physicists are eager to study. Although these particles are not visible, it is possible to see where they have been, using a device called a bubble chamber.

The bubble chamber contains liquid hydrogen that is pressurized so it is on the verge of boiling. Wherever subatomic particles pass through the liquid hydrogen, they give it just enough extra energy to boil. This produces a trail of tiny hydrogen gas bubbles, which follows the particles. The physicists photograph the trails to help them with their research.

Liquid hydrogen is used in bubble chambers. These devices allow scientists to study the strange spiral paths taken by tiny subatomic particles. ▶

Into space with liquid hydrogen

Car manufacturers are experimenting with liquid hydrogen as a fuel for cars. Although it is difficult to store and handle, scientists are confident they can overcome these problems. However, rockets and spacecraft have used liquid hydrogen as a fuel for many years.

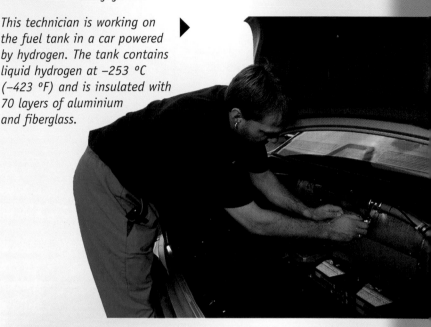

This technician is working on the fuel tank in a car powered by hydrogen. The tank contains liquid hydrogen at −253 °C (−423 °F) and is insulated with 70 layers of aluminium and fiberglass.

The space shuttles use liquid hydrogen to power their main engines. The external tank attached to the shuttle at liftoff contains 1.5 million liters (1.59 million quarts) of it. There are also 500,000 liters (528,344 quarts) of liquid oxygen stored inside the nose of the tank. The two liquids are mixed and ignite in the engines, producing huge forces that push the shuttle into space. The tank itself is made from a strong, but light, aluminum-lithium alloy.

Cold cracks

The shuttle fleet was grounded for repairs in 2002. Very small cracks were found in the tubes that supply liquid hydrogen to the engines. These could cause a piece of metal to come off the tubes and destroy the engines. No cracks were found in the tubes supplying the liquid oxygen and it seemed that the extreme cold of the liquid hydrogen was to blame.

A Hydrogen Economy

Hydrogen is easy to set on fire, and it burns with a hot flame. A small amount of hydrogen releases a lot of energy—nearly three times more than the same mass of natural gas or oil. Hydrogen has other advantages too, but there are some disadvantages.

Environmentally friendly hydrogen

Fossil fuels, such as natural gas and oil, produce carbon dioxide and water when they burn. However, when hydrogen burns, it produces only water vapor. This gives hydrogen a big advantage over fossil fuels. This is because carbon dioxide is a greenhouse gas that traps heat in the atmosphere and contributes to global warming. However, fossil fuels are still used despite because hydrogen is difficult to transport and store safely.

Hydrogen for homes and cars

Hydrogen gas could be piped to homes for heating and cooking, just like natural gas. However, this is not practical for cars. If hydrogen gas is stored under pressure, more gas can be squeezed into a small volume. Unfortunately, special containers are needed to do this.

If hydrogen gas is cooled below −253 °C (−423 °F), it condenses and becomes a liquid. However, about a quarter of the energy contained in the hydrogen would be used just to keep it that cold and special containers would still be needed for storage. Despite these problems, hydrogen is already being used to power some vehicles.

Metal hydrides

One possible answer to the problems of storing hydrogen safely and cheaply involves metal hydrides. These are produced when some metals react with hydrogen. Alloys, such as magnesium-nickel and magnesium-copper, can store large amounts of hydrogen this way. When the metal hydrides are heated, they release the hydrogen gas. However, more scientific research is needed to increase the amount of hydrogen the alloys can store.

The hydrogen fuel cell

In 1842 Sir William Grove, an English scientist, invented the gas battery. Grove's invention consisted of two strips of platinum metal half-covered by sulphuric acid. He discovered that electricity was produced if hydrogen was passed over one strip and oxygen over the other. The gas battery is the basis of the modern hydrogen fuel cell.

The hydrogen fuel cell produces electricity from hydrogen and oxygen when it is supplied in a steady stream. The only product is water vapor, making it very attractive as an environmentally friendly power source. The International Space Station uses fuel cells to make electricity, and drinking water is a useful by-product for the astronauts. Back on Earth, hydrogen fuel cells are being used to power cars and other vehicles. The electricity they generate charges a battery that powers an electric motor.

◀ *Oil and natural gas produce water and carbon dioxide (a greenhouse gas) when they burn. They may also produce black smoke (opposite). However, when hydrogen burns the only product is water vapor.*

CHAPTER 5

Hydrogen Oxide

When hydrogen and oxygen react together, the only product is water. Like all compounds, water is very different from the elements it contains. Hydrogen and oxygen are both gases at room temperature, whereas water is a liquid. Pure water freezes at 0 °C (32 °F) and boils at 100 °C (212 °F). It is colorless and does not have an odor. Tap water usually smells faintly of chlorine because chlorine is added to kill harmful bacteria.

Hydrogen oxide, better known as water, is the most abundant compound on the surface of Earth. As a result, when seen from space, Earth is a very watery place covered with oceans and clouds. ▶

Water is the most abundant compound on Earth, and covers 71 percent of Earth's surface. There are about 1,400 million cubic kilometers of water on Earth. This is so much that if each person in the world scooped out a liter (quart) of water every second, it would take 7,000 years to drain the oceans!

It's a liquid, but is it water?

There are two simple chemical tests to see if a liquid is water. If it is added to very dry copper sulphate crystals, they change from white to blue. Paper soaked in cobalt chloride solution can also be used as a test for water. Cobalt chloride paper is blue when dry, but turns pink when it is damp with water. Even the moisture from your fingers is enough to change its color.

Burst pipes

Most substances contract when they change from a liquid to a solid, but water expands when it freezes. A kilogram (2.2 pounds) of water has a volume of 1.00 liter (1 quart), but ice expands and fills 1.09 liters (1.15 quarts). If water freezes in a pipe, it not only blocks it, but expands and pushes against the inside of the pipe, causing it to crack. When the weather becomes warmer, the ice melts, unblocking the pipe, and water leaks out of the crack.

Icebergs

Ice is less dense than water, which is why ice cubes float in a drink. The density of pure water is 1.00 g/cm³ but seawater can be nearly 1.03 g/cm³ because it contains dissolved salt. Meanwhile, the density of icebergs varies from just 0.86 g/cm³ to 0.92 g/cm³, so they float in the sea. About 90 percent of an iceberg is underwater and many ships, including the famous *Titanic*, have collided with sharp pieces of iceberg underwater and sunk.

▼ *People often talk about things being "just the tip of the iceberg." Ice is less dense than water, so it floats, but only about 10 percent of an iceberg is visible on the surface.*

Water the dissolver

Water is a good solvent, which means that many substances dissolve in it easily. All sorts of substances will dissolve in water, such as sugar and sodium chloride (common salt). On average, every liter (quart) of seawater contains 26 grams of dissolved sodium chloride, which adds up to 35,000 trillion tons in all of Earth's seas and oceans.

Water Everywhere

When Earth was first formed, it was very hot. Volcanoes threw huge amounts of gases such as carbon dioxide and steam into the air. Eventually Earth's temperature cooled to below 100 °C (212 °F), and the steam condensed to form liquid water, which fell as rain and formed the oceans.

Scientists believe that similar things happened on Venus and Mars, but neither planet has liquid water now. Venus is closer to the Sun than Earth is, and it is too hot there for steam to condense. It is likely that chemical reactions split the water molecules into hydrogen and oxygen gas. Hydrogen has very small molecules that can move extremely quickly and they probably escaped into space. Mars is further away from the Sun than Earth is and is too cold for liquid water. However, space probes have discovered some frozen water under the surface. Scientists believe that Mars had oceans, rivers, and floods over three billion years ago, before it cooled.

▲
This is the Valles Marineris canyon on Mars, which scientists believe was carved out by water millions of years ago. Although there is no flowing water on Mars now, the Mars Odyssey *space probe discovered in 2003 that the soil on Mars contains an average of 6.5 percent water.*

Before the ozone layer

The Earth's ozone layer protects living things from harmful ultraviolet light. Before it formed 400 million years ago, life could only exist in the oceans. This is because seawater gives some protection from the Sun's ultraviolet light.

The water cycle

Earth's water is continually moving and changing. Water evaporates from the surface of lakes and seas, forming water vapor. This rises into the air and becomes cooler. As the water vapor cools, it condenses into clouds of tiny water droplets. When the clouds cool further, like they do when they rise over mountains, the droplets clump together, eventually becoming large enough to fall as rain. Most rain just falls back into the sea, but about a fifth of it falls over the land. It then flows back to the sea over ground as rivers and underground as groundwater. These processes are driven by heat energy from the Sun, forming the water cycle. All of the water in Earth's atmosphere is recycled 33 times every year!

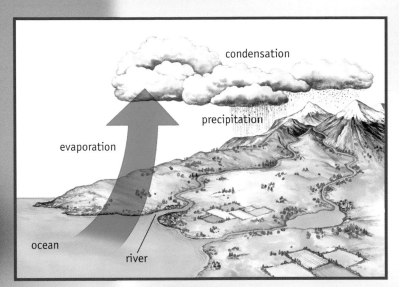

This diagram shows the water cycle, in which water is continually recycled between the oceans, clouds, and land. The water cycle is driven by heat energy from the Sun.

Swimming pools and mild weather

Water has a high heat capacity, which means a large amount of energy is needed to warm it, making swimming pools expensive to heat. However, warm water stores a lot of heat energy, so oceans affect the kind of weather places get. Oceans absorb heat in the summer and release it in the winter, preventing large swings in temperature. For example, the average yearly temperatures in England, which is an island, only vary by about 10 °C (50 °F). On a large continent like North America, areas away from the sea can have average yearly temperatures that vary by as much as 40 °C (104 °F).

Water and Living Things

Without water, Earth would be a lifeless planet. About 60 percent of your body mass is water, and you can survive only a few days without it.

Photosynthesis and respiration

Plants make their own food using a process called photosynthesis. Energy from sunlight enables carbon dioxide and water to react together to produce sugar and oxygen. If a plant does not get enough water, its cells become floppy. The plant wilts and may eventually die.

Respiration is the chemical reaction that all cells use to release energy from food. Water is a product of respiration. Your body gets rid of extra water by sweating or going to the toilet. Your breath contains water vapor, which you can see when it condenses in the cold air as you breathe out. Without respiration you could not get the energy you need for your body to move, grow, and keep warm.

Water is vital to stay alive. People usually take safe and clean drinking water for granted, but in many parts of the world it is very difficult to get. ▶

Germination

Seeds may look dead, but they are just dormant. This means that all the chemical processes in their cells, such as respiration, are happening very slowly. When seeds are put into damp soil, they soak up water. The cells begin to respire more quickly, and the seed germinates. Germinating seeds use their stored food to produce roots and shoots, forming new plants. Without water, seeds cannot germinate.

Freshwater

Although there is a large amount of water on Earth, about 97 percent of it is seawater, and very little of the remainder is fit to drink. Most of it is locked away as ice in glaciers and icebergs or below ground as groundwater. Nearly all drinking water comes from rivers, and they only contain 0.0001 percent of the world's water! The rivers also supply the water needed for industrial processes, such as steelmaking. Over 200 tons of water are used to make each ton of steel.

Clean water

To survive, a person needs about five liters of water a day from food and drink, but uses at least ten times that for other purposes such as washing. In the industrialized nations, clean water is taken for granted, but over one billion people in the world cannot get it. Contaminated water causes over 4 billion cases of diarrhea each year, killing over 2 million people. Many tropical diseases are spread by parasites that live in untreated water. Schistosomiasis (pronounced shis-toe-so-my-a-siss) is a tropical disease caused by tiny worms that live in the veins around the liver and intestines. People become infected if they touch infested water, for example, when they irrigate fields, collect drinking water, wash themselves, or go swimming. About 200 million people are infected, mainly in central and southern Africa. In 2002, the World Summit for Sustainable Development agreed to take steps to halve the proportion of people without safe drinking water by 2015.

◀ *Clean running water is difficult to find in some developing countries and war zones, so people may have to travel many miles to collect water. Even then, it may be dirty and capable of causing fatal diseases such as cholera.*

Water and Electricity

The electric battery was invented by Alessandro Volta, an Italian scientist. When he announced his invention in 1800, chemists rushed to find out what would happen when electricity is passed through chemicals. One of the first chemicals they tested was water.

Only a few months after Volta announced his invention, William Nicholson, an English chemist, discovered that water splits into hydrogen and oxygen when electricity is passed through. Although the small amount of electricity from a battery is usually safe, it is extremely dangerous to pass electricity from an outlet through water, and you must never try this at home. Water is a poor conductor of electricity unless large voltages are applied, but it conducts better if some acid is added.

The electrolysis of water

When electricity is used to split up a compound into simpler substances, the process is called electrolysis. Water is a compound made from hydrogen and oxygen atoms. Water molecules split up to make hydrogen ions, H^+ and hydroxide ions, OH^-. Ions are electrically charged particles, so the hydrogen ions are attracted to the negative electrode and become hydrogen gas. The hydroxide ions are attracted to the positive electrode, where they react with each other to form oxygen gas and water.

water

*Water can be split into ▶
hydrogen and oxygen using
electricity. The gases bubble
out of the water into test
tubes, where they can be
collected. The test tube on
the right contains hydrogen
and the one on the left
contains oxygen.*

platinum
electrode

H^+

OH^-

The equation for the electrolysis of water is:

$$\text{water} \xrightarrow{\text{electricity}} \text{hydrogen} + \text{oxygen}$$

$$2H_2O \xrightarrow{\text{electricity}} 2H_2 + O_2$$

Twice as much hydrogen is made compared to oxygen because each water molecule has two hydrogen atoms, but only one oxygen atom.

Industrial hydrogen

Most hydrogen is extracted by reacting steam with coal or natural gas. Unfortunately, these reactions also produce carbon dioxide gas, which is a contributor to global warming. In addition coal and natural gas are both fossil fuels that will run out one day. Obtaining hydrogen through the electrolysis of water is a good alternative, although electricity is expensive to produce and is often generated from fossil fuels too.

Solar cells convert the Sun's light directly into electricity. Electricity can also be generated using alternative energy sources such as hydroelectric power, wind, and waves. The cost of electricity will decrease when these alternative sources become more widely used. Then the electrolysis of water will be a more economic way of extracting hydrogen.

◀ *This wave power station on the Scottish island of Islay generates inexpensive electricity. Cheap electricity is needed to make the electrolysis of hydrogen economic.*

Hydrogen from the chlor-alkali industry

Hydrogen is a by-product of the chlor-alkali industry. This chemical industry extracts chlorine and sodium hydroxide by passing electricity through sodium chloride solution.

Corrosive Hydrogen

Acids

When acids dissolve in water they make acidic solutions. All acids contain hydrogen atoms, which give off hydrogen gas when they react with metals. Vinegar is a weak acid that contains acetic acid, CH_3COOH, while lemon juice has citric acid, $C_6H_8O_7$. People's stomachs contain hydrochloric acid, HCl, which is a strong acid that kills harmful bacteria in food as well as helping us to digest proteins. There are also strong acids in car batteries (sulphuric acid, H_2SO_4) and in cola drinks (phosphoric acid, H_3PO_4). This is why cola drinks dissolve our teeth.

◀ Lemons like these, and other citrus fruits, contain a weak acid called citric acid.

◀ Bottles of very strong or concentrated acids are labelled with this hazard symbol. It warns that the chemical is corrosive and can attack living tissues such as the skin or eyes.

Weak or diluted acids are less ▶ dangerous than strong or concentrated acids, but they can still harm you if they are spilt on the skin or swallowed. This hazard symbol warns if a chemical is an irritant.

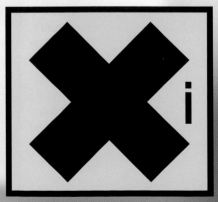

Fizzing furiously

Metals react with acids to produce a salt and hydrogen.

> The word equation for the reaction between a metal and an acid is:
>
> metal + acid → salt + hydrogen

> These are some examples of reactions between metals and acids. See how the salt gets its name.
>
> zinc + sulphuric acid → zinc sulphate + hydrogen
>
> $Zn(s) + H_2SO_4(aq) → ZnSO_4(aq) + H_2(g)$
>
> magnesium + hydrochloric acid → magnesium chloride + hydrogen
>
> $Mg(s) + 2HCl(aq) → MgCl_2(aq) + H_2(g)$

The names of salts are somewhat like your name. They have a first name and a last name. The first name is the name of the metal and the last name comes from the acid used. For example, the last name is nitrate if nitric acid is used and phosphate if phosphoric acid is used. When a salt is made with hydrochloric acid, the last part of the salt's name is chloride.

Metals can be arranged in order of their reactivity to make a list called a reactivity series. Metals above hydrogen react with acids, while those below normally do not. The more reactive the metal, the bigger the reaction. For example, you could make table salt, or sodium chloride, by reacting sodium with hydrochloric acid, but the reaction would be violent because sodium is very reactive! To make it safely, you need a different type of substance, called a base.

element

most reactive

potassium
sodium
lithium
calcium
magnesium
aluminium
zinc
iron
tin
lead
hydrogen
copper
silver
gold
platinum

least reactive

◀ A reactivity series of metals with hydrogen included.

Bases and Alkalis

Bases are substances that react with acids and neutralize them, so they are no longer acidic. If a base dissolves in water, it is also called an alkali. This means that all alkalis are bases, but not all bases are alkalis. Sodium oxide powder is a base because it neutralizes acids. It also dissolves in water, so it is an alkali.

Back to base

Lots of substances are bases, including ammonia, metal oxides such as copper oxide, and metal hydroxides like sodium hydroxide. Metal carbonates and metal bicarbonates are bases, too. These include substances such as calcium carbonate, which is found in chalk and limestone, and sodium hydrogen carbonate, which is part of baking powder.

Alkali and alkaline

For thousands of years people have burned plants and boiled their ashes in water to produce an alkaline solution. The word *alkali* comes from *al-qali*, which is Arabic for "burned ashes." Potassium hydroxide, KOH, is a common alkali. Potassium gets its name from *potash,* which means "the ashes from a pot." People sometimes get alkali and alkaline confused. Remember that acids dissolve in water to make acidic solutions and alkalis dissolve in water to make alkaline solutions. Boiling fats and oils in an alkaline solution makes soap.

Soapy alkalis

Alkalis must be handled carefully because they are corrosive or harmful, like acids. Alkalis react with the natural oils in your skin to produce soap, which is why they feel soapy! However, alkalis can cause nasty burns, so they must be washed off your skin and clothes. They are particularly dangerous if they get into your eyes, so you must wear eye protection when you do experiments with alkalis.

Bases and salts

A salt is always produced when a base reacts with an acid and is named in the same way as a salt made from a metal and an acid. For example, sodium chloride is made from the reaction between sodium hydroxide and hydrochloric acid. The other chemicals produced depend on the type of base used. Water will be formed if the base is a metal oxide or hydroxide, while water and carbon dioxide will be produced if a metal carbonate or hydrogen carbonate is used.

The word equations for the reactions between different bases and acids are:

metal oxide + acid → salt + water

metal hydroxide + acid → salt + water

metal carbonate + acid → salt + water + carbon dioxide

metal hydrogencarbonate + acid → salt + water + carbon dioxide

When ammonia solution reacts with an acid, the first part of the name for the salt formed is ammonium. For instance, ammonia solution reacts with hydrochloric acid to make ammonium chloride and water.

◀ *Acids and alkalis react together to form a salt and water. When the fumes from concentrated hydrochloric acid meet the fumes from ammonia solution, they react to form clouds of white ammonium chloride and water vapor.*

Indicators and the pH Scale

There are several different ways to find out if a solution is acidic or alkaline.

Indicators

Indicators are substances that can tell whether a solution is acidic, alkaline, or neutral by their color. Litmus is an indicator that is extracted from lichens. Lichens are formed from a fungus and an alga, which grow on tree trunks and rocks. Litmus solution turns red in acids and blue in alkalis. Universal indicator is a mixture of different indicators. It not only turns red in acids and blue in alkalis, but it turns green in neutral solutions and shows you the strength of an acidic or alkaline solution.

Litmus paper versus universal indicator paper

This table shows the color changes made by indicator papers in different solutions.

	acidic	neutral	alkaline
red litmus paper	stays red	stays red	turns blue
blue litmus paper	turns red	stays blue	stays blue
universal indicator paper	turns red	turns green	turns blue

Litmus paper is not as useful as universal indicator paper. You may need both a red and a blue piece of litmus paper to be sure of your result, and litmus paper cannot tell you if an acid or alkali is strong or weak.

◀ *Blue litmus paper turns red when it soaks up the acidic juice from a lemon.*

The pH scale

The pH scale is a measure of acidity. It runs from 0 to 14. Solutions that have pH numbers less than 7 are acidic. So alkaline solutions have pH numbers greater than 7. The pH number of neutral solutions is exactly 7. Strong acids have pH numbers near 0, and strong alkalis have pH numbers near 14. Weak acids and alkalis have pH numbers close to 7. Pure water is neutral.

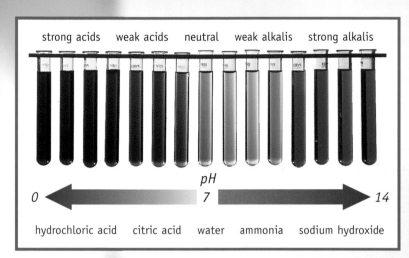

◄ The solutions in these test tubes show the universal indicator pH scale.

strong acids   weak acids   neutral   weak alkalis   strong alkalis

pH

0 ◄──────────────── 7 ────────────────► 14

hydrochloric acid   citric acid   water   ammonia   sodium hydroxide

The pH value of a solution can be found using universal indicator paper and a color chart, where each color is given a pH number. A device called a pH meter can also be used. A probe is put into the liquid to be tested, and the pH number is read on the scale.

Neutralization and the pH scale

When a base neutralizes an acid, it is called a neutralization reaction. It is the reaction between hydrogen ions from the acid and hydroxide ions from the base. These ions join together to form water. The pH scale is an inverse measure of the amount of hydrogen ions dissolved in the solution. This means strong acids produce a lot of hydrogen ions, giving a low pH number.

The equation for the neutralization reaction is:

hydrogen ions + hydroxide ions ⟶ water

$$H^+ + OH^- \rightarrow H_2O$$

Caves and Cooking

Limestone and chalk are almost pure forms of calcium carbonate, $CaCO_3$. Calcium carbonate is a base, so it can react with acids and neutralize them. You can test a rock to see if calcium carbonate is present by adding a few drops of hydrochloric acid. If it contains limestone or chalk, the rock immediately begins to fizz. This is because the reaction produces carbon dioxide gas.

The equation for the reaction between calcium carbonate and hydrochloric acid is:

calcium carbonate + hydrochloric acid $\rightarrow$ calcium chloride + water + carbon dioxide

$$CaCO_3(s) + 2HCl(aq) \rightarrow CaCl_2(aq) + H_2O(l) + CO_2(g)$$

Rainwater is naturally acidic because carbon dioxide in the air dissolves in it, forming a weak acid called carbonic acid, H_2CO_3. When rainwater falls on limestone or chalk, it reacts with the calcium carbonate, producing calcium hydrogen carbonate, which can dissolve in water. This causes the rock to wear away, and over thousands of years channels and caves are formed. When water that contains calcium hydrogen carbonate drips from cave ceilings it evaporates, leaving behind stalactites and stalagmites of calciumcarbonate.

The equation for the reaction between calcium carbonate and carbonic acid is:

calcium carbonate + carbonic acid $\rightleftharpoons$ calcium hydrogen carbonate

$$CaCO_3(s) + H_2CO_3(aq) \rightleftharpoons Ca(HCO_3)_2(aq)$$

This is a reversible reaction, because calcium hydrogencarbonate can break down again to form calcium carbonate and carbonic acid. Instead of the usual arrow, the $\rightleftharpoons$ symbol is used.

Acid rain

Cars and factories produce polluting gases that include sulfur dioxide and nitrogen oxides, or NOx. These gases dissolve in the clouds, and the rain that later falls from them is more acidic than normal. Acid rain is very damaging to statues and buildings made from limestone or marble.

Baking soda

Sodium hydrogen carbonate, $NaHCO_3$, is often called baking soda or bicarbonate of soda. It dissolves in water to form a weak alkaline solution. Some toothpastes contain baking soda, which helps to neutralize acid made by bacteria in the mouths from the sugars in food. The tiny baking soda crystals also help to clean teeth.

Baking soda breaks down when it is heated and releases carbon dioxide gas. This helps cakes to rise in the oven. Baking soda is often mixed with a dry acid such as tartaric acid to make baking powder. When baking powder is put into a damp cake mixture, the sodium hydrogen carbonate and tartaric acid react and release carbon dioxide.

The equation for the breakdown of baking soda when it is heated is:

$$\text{sodium hydrogen carbonate} \xrightarrow{\text{heat}} \text{sodium carbonate} + \text{water} + \text{carbon dioxide}$$

$$2NaHCO_3(s) \xrightarrow{\text{heat}} Na_2CO_3(s) + H_2O(l) + CO_2(g)$$

The equation for damp baking powder releasing carbon dioxide is:

$$\text{sodium hydrogen carbonate} + \text{tartaric acid} \longrightarrow \text{sodium tartrate} + \text{water} + \text{carbon dioxide}$$

$$2NaHCO_3(aq) + C_4H_6O_6(aq) \rightarrow Na_2C_4H_4O_6(aq) + 2H_2O(l) + 2CO_2(g)$$

Big Bases

Some of the bases and alkalis that you use in school laboratories are produced in huge amounts on an industrial scale. These include calcium oxide, sodium hydroxide, and ammonia.

Calcium oxide

Calcium oxide is made by strongly heating calcium carbonate. Rocks such as limestone and dolomite are almost pure calcium carbonate. Over a hundred million tons of calcium oxide are produced from them each year.

> *The equation for making calcium oxide from calcium carbonate is:*
>
> calcium carbonate $\rightarrow$ calcium oxide + carbon dioxide
>
> $$CaCO_3(s) \rightarrow CaO(s) + CO_2(g)$$
>
> *This is called a decomposition reaction because the calcium carbonate breaks down to form new substances.*

Calcium oxide is a base because it reacts with acids and neutralizes them. It is often called lime. Farmers spread lime on their fields to neutralize excess acid in the soil, helping their crops to grow better. Builders join bricks together using mortar, which is a mixture of lime, sand, and water.

This lake in Sweden is polluted by acid rain. The acidity kills the fish and releases poisonous metals from the ground. To reduce the lake's acidity, many thousands of tons of calcium oxide powder are sprayed into it. ▶

Cement is made from lime and clay heated together. Concrete is a mixture of lime, sand, small stones, and water. Calcium oxide is also used to purify iron and steel. It reacts with acidic impurities in the melted iron, forming waste that is easily removed.

Sodium hydroxide

Sodium hydroxide is made by passing electricity through concentrated sodium chloride solution. The electricity splits the sodium chloride into its two elements. Sodium forms at the negative electrode, where it reacts with water to form sodium hydroxide and hydrogen gas. Meanwhile, chlorine gas forms at the positive electrode. This is easy to do in the laboratory but harder to do on an industrial scale because hydrogen and chlorine will react together if they meet. Over 40 million tons of sodium hydroxide are made each year. It has all sorts of uses, including the manufacture of paper, artificial fibers, and chemicals, as well as for neutralizing the sulfuric acid used by oil refineries.

Ammonia

Ammonia is made using the Haber process. Nitrogen and hydrogen are forced to react together at 200 times atmospheric pressure. The rate of the reaction is increased using an iron catalyst and by raising the temperature to about 450 °C (842 °F).

The equation for the Haber process is:

$$\text{nitrogen} + \text{hydrogen} \rightleftharpoons \text{ammonia}$$

$$N_2(g) + 3H_2(g) \rightleftharpoons 2NH_3(g)$$

This reaction does not go to completion. It is reversible, so we use the $\rightleftharpoons$ symbol instead of an arrow.

Over 100 million tons of ammonia are made each year. Most of it is used in fertilizers, but it has many other uses that include the manufacture of explosives, plastics, and artificial fibers such as nylon.

Big Acids

The acids that you use in school laboratories are also produced in huge amounts on an industrial scale.

Nitric acid

Nitric acid is made by the Ostwald process. Ammonia and air are passed over a hot platinum-rhodium catalyst, producing nitrogen monoxide gas and steam. Then the nitrogen monoxide reacts with water and more oxygen to form nitric acid.

> The equations for some of the stages in the Ostwald process are:
>
> ammonia + oxygen $\rightarrow$ nitrogen monoxide + steam
>
> $$4NH_3(g) + 5O_2(g) \rightarrow 4NO(g) + 6H_2O(g)$$
>
> nitrogen monoxide + oxygen + water $\rightarrow$ nitric acid
>
> $$4NO(g) + 3O_2(g) + 2H_2O(l) \rightarrow 4HNO_3(aq)$$

About 60 million tons of nitric acid are made each year. Most of it is used to produce ammonium nitrate, a compound found in fertilizers and explosives. Nitric acid is also used to make dyes, plastics, and explosives, such as nitroglycerine and trinitrotoluene (TNT).

Sulfuric acid

Sulfuric acid is made by the Contact process, which happens in three stages. Sulfur is burned in air to produce sulfur dioxide gas. Then, at a temperature of 450 °C (842 °F), twice normal atmospheric pressure and using a catalyst called vanadium pentoxide, it is reacted with more air to make sulfur trioxide gas. Finally, sulfur trioxide reacts with water to make sulfuric acid.

More sulfuric acid is made than any other chemical—about 150 million tons worldwide each year! Most of it is used to make fertilizers, but it is also used to make plastics, paints, and explosives.

Phosphoric acid

Phosphoric acid is made by reacting phosphate rock with sulfuric acid. Nearly all of the 35 million tons made each year are used to make fertilizers. However, phosphoric acid has other uses, which include making water softeners for detergents and rust-proofing steel. It is also used to flavor cola drinks.

Hydrochloric acid

Hydrochloric acid is usually made as a by-product of other chemical processes, although hydrogen and chlorine can be reacted together to make hydrogen chloride gas. This is cooled and dissolved in water to make hydrochloric acid. Hydrochloric acid is used to clean metals and circuit boards, as well as making bleaches, dyes, and solvents.

◀ *Hydrogen gas is made when metals react with water or acids. Here you can see lots of tiny bubbles of hydrogen being released when zinc reacts with hydrochloric acid.*

Hydrogen in Complex Molecules

When hydrogen atoms join with atoms such as oxygen and sulfur they form simple molecules, but when they bond with carbon atoms they can make very complex molecules. This is because carbon atoms often join together to make long chains, branches, and rings. Molecules made from hydrogen and carbon atoms are called hydrocarbons.

Hydrocarbons from oil and natural gas

Nearly all the hydrocarbons come from oil and natural gas. These are usually deep underground and have to be drilled. Oil is a mixture of many different hydrocarbons, including solids and gases dissolved in a thick mixture of liquids. The crude oil must be separated into different parts, or fractions, at an oil refinery so that they can be used.

A fishy tale

Millions of years ago, sea creatures died and were buried under layers of mineral sediments. Their bodies did not rot because oxygen could not reach them. Instead, they were squashed by the weight of the sediments and heated. Eventually the mineral sediments became rock and the remains turned into oil and natural gas.

The different hydrocarbons are separated from each other in a metal tower called a fractionating column. The fractions from the top of the column are gases with very small molecules, those from the middle are liquids with medium-sized molecules, and those at the bottom are solids with big molecules. Each fraction contains hydrocarbons called alkanes.

Alkanes

The carbon atoms of alkanes are joined to each other with single bonds. The fraction from the top of the fractionating column contains the fuel gases: methane, ethane, propane, and butane. Methane, CH_4, is the simplest alkane. Each molecule contains four hydrogen atoms joined to a carbon atom. Natural gas is mostly methane with some ethane.

Natural gas is an important fuel for power stations, factories, and homes. Propane and butane are used in bottled gases, such as those used for camping.

◀ *Butane gas, extracted from crude oil at oil refineries and stored under pressure in metal cylinders, is widely used by campers for cooking and lighting.*

How many bonds?

When two carbon atoms join together using one chemical bond, it is called a single bond. Carbon atoms can also join together using two or three chemical bonds, called double bonds and triple bonds respectively.

Most of the other fractions are liquids that are used to make lubricating oil and fuels. Gasoline and diesel oil are important fuels for cars and trucks, while kerosene is used in jet fuel. Fuel oil is a very thick liquid used by ships and oil-fired power stations.

Very long alkanes, such as paraffin waxes and bitumen, are solid at room temperature. Each molecule of bitumen contains over 50 carbon atoms and over 100 hydrogen atoms. Candles and polishes are made from paraffin waxes, and bitumen is used to surface roads.

◀ *Jet aircraft are powered by kerosene, a liquid fuel extracted from crude oil.*

Plastic and Margarine

Medium-sized alkanes, such as octane, are often more useful than big alkanes, such as bitumen. However, crude oil has too few medium-sized alkanes and too many big alkanes. Some of the big alkanes are broken into smaller alkanes using a process called cracking, which involves heating them under pressure or passing them over a catalyst. Cracking also produces a different type of hydrocarbon called an alkene.

Alkenes

In an alkene molecule, two or more of the carbon atoms are joined together using double bonds instead of single bonds. This makes alkenes more reactive than alkanes. Hydrogen, bromine, water, and other chemicals can join with alkenes wherever there is a double bond. Alkenes can even join on to each other to make really long molecules, called addition polymers. Poly means "many."

Testing for alkenes

Bromine mixed with water is used to test if hydrocarbons are alkanes or alkenes. Bromine water stays brown when it is shaken with an alkane, but becomes colorless when mixed with an alkene. This is because bromine atoms add on to the alkene molecules.

Addition polymers

There are lots of addition polymers, depending on the alkene used to make them. The simplest alkene is ethene, C_2H_4. When ethene molecules join end-to-end, they make polyethene (many ethenes), which is used to make plastic bags. The next simplest alkene is propene, C_3H_6. When propene molecules join end-to-end they make polypropene, another type of plastic that is used to make tough polypropylene ropes and crates. Styrene is a more complex alkene with a ring of carbon and hydrogen atoms. When styrene molecules join end-to-end they make polystyrene, which is used for fast-food containers and TV cabinets.

▲

Polystyrene is a plastic made from a complex molecule containing rings of carbon and hydrogen atoms. It is widely used to make packaging and containers for food.

Margarine

Hydrogen can add onto the double bonds in alkenes. When this happens, it converts the alkene into an alkane. This might seem pointless, but it is an important step in making margarine.

Oils and fats are made from molecules with long chains of carbon atoms. If all the carbon atoms are joined together by single bonds, the fat is called saturated. Saturated fats, such as lard, are hard solids at room temperature. If some of the carbon atoms are joined together by double bonds, the fat is called unsaturated. Unsaturated fats are soft solids or runny oils, such as vegetable oil.

If hydrogen is added to vegetable oils, they become more saturated. This makes them solid rather than liquid. Margarine manufacturers react vegetable oils with hydrogen gas using a nickel catalyst, which converts some of the double bonds into single bonds. This is the process involved in making hydrogenated vegetable oil. The different products from the reaction are blended together to make different margarines for cooking or spreading.

Ethanol and Esters

The liquid ethanol, C_2H_5OH, is the best known member of a whole family of compounds named alcohols and is commonly called alcohol. Around 30 billion liters of ethanol are made in the world each year, but most of this does not end up in alcoholic drinks! Ethanol is a very good fuel and is used as a solvent in deodorants, perfumes, and ink.

The hydroxyl group

Every alcohol contains a hydroxyl group, OH, which is an oxygen atom and a hydrogen atom joined together. Without it, alcohols would not be alcohols at all.

Making ethanol

Ethanol can be made from ethene, an alkene formed by cracking oil fractions. To make ethanol, the ethene must be mixed with steam at 60 times atmospheric pressure (atm), heated to 300 °C (572 °F) and then passed over a catalyst.

The equation for making ethanol from ethene and steam is:

$$\text{ethene + steam} \xrightarrow{\text{300 °C, 60atm}} \text{ethanol}$$

$$C_2H_4(g) + H_2O(g) \xrightarrow{\text{300 °C, 60atm}} C_2H_5OH(l)$$

Phosphoric acid stuck onto solid pellets is used as a catalyst.

Ethanol can also be made from sugar. Yeast is a type of single-celled fungi that breaks up sugar, using fermentation. This process involves natural catalysts called enzymes. Fermentation produces ethanol and carbon dioxide gas. Almost anything containing sugar can be used for fermentation, including grape juice, sugarcane, and corn.

The equation for fermentation is:

$$\text{glucose} \xrightarrow{\text{enzymes in yeast}} \text{ethanol + carbon dioxide}$$

$$C_6H_{12}O_6(aq) \xrightarrow{\text{enzymes in yeast}} 2C_2H_5OH(aq) + 2CO_2(g)$$

◀ Yeast can ferment sugar solution to produce
the ethanol contained in beer and wine.
The reaction also produces bubbles of carbon
dioxide gas, which causes foam to form on the
surface of the sugar solution.

Ethanol the biofuel

Crude oil is a limited resource because it
takes millions of years to form and once it
is used up it will be gone for good. Ethanol
is a biofuel that can be made from various
crops that can be replaced. Huge amounts
of ethanol are made in Brazil from
sugarcane and in the United States from
corn. Gasohol, a mixture of 10 percent
ethanol and 90 percent gasoline, fuels
many cars in Brazil, while in the United States a mixture of
85 percent ethanol and 15 percent gasoline, called E85, does
a similar job.

Fruity smells

If a bottle of wine is left open, the ethanol in it reacts with
oxygen in the air, turning it into acetic acid, CH_3COOH. This
is a weak acid that belongs to a family of compounds named
carboxylic acids. Vinegar is four percent acetic acid, which is
why it has a sharp taste.

When an alcohol and a carboxylic acid react together, they
make water and a complex substance called an ester. Esters
have fruity tastes and smells and are found naturally in fruit
and flowers. Different combinations of alcohols and
carboxylic acids make different esters. Manufacturers add
esters to cosmetics and shampoos to give them a natural
fragrance. Esters are used as artificial flavors in yogurts and
other foods.

Carbohydrates Everywhere

Animals obtain their food by eating plants or other animals, but plants make their own food through a process called photosynthesis. Using the energy from sunlight, water reacts with carbon dioxide to produce glucose and oxygen. Glucose is just one sugar in a large range of compounds that includes big, complex molecules, such as starch. These compounds are called carbohydrates because they contain carbon, hydrogen, and oxygen.

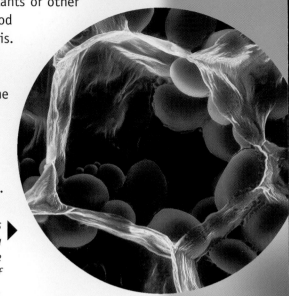

These highly magnified potato cells contain rounded granules of starch, a complex carbohydrate used as a food store by plants. Carbohydrates are compounds of carbon, hydrogen, and oxygen.

The equation for photosynthesis is:

$$\text{carbon dioxide} + \text{water} \xrightarrow{\text{sunlight}} \text{glucose} + \text{oxygen}$$

$$6CO_2(g) + 6H_2O(l) \xrightarrow{\text{sunlight}} C_6H_{12}O_6(s) + 6O_2(g)$$

Photosynthesis takes place in tiny green bodies in plant cells called chloroplasts.

Sugar, sugar

Glucose and galactose are two simple sugars. They both have the formula $C_6H_{12}O_6$, but they are not identical. Other simple sugars also have the same chemical formula but different arrangements of their atoms. Two molecules of a simple sugar can join together to make more complex sugars. For example, glucose added to galactose forms lactose, which is found in milk, while glucose attached to fructose makes sucrose, which is cane sugar.

Starch is made when thousands of glucose molecules join together. Plants store their food as tiny starch granules in their cells. Glucose is the main sugar in our blood, but we store it in the liver and muscles as glycogen. This is another complex molecule made from thousands of glucose molecules that are joined together in a different way to the molecules in starch.

Blood groups

In 1901, Karl Landsteiner first discovered that there are different types of blood, which he named A, B, and O. Each blood group has a different chain of sugar molecules on the surface of the red blood cells.

Cellulose—the tough stuff

Cellulose is a tough molecule found in plant cell walls that is made from glucose molecules joined together in yet another way. People can digest starch but not cellulose because they do not have the necessary enzymes. However, many fungi and bacteria do have these enzymes and use cellulose for food. Cows and other ruminants have bacteria in their stomachs that can digest the cellulose in plants.

The cellulose in wood is used to make paper and an artificial fiber called rayon. To make rayon, the cellulose is turned into a syrupy substance called viscose by reacting it with sodium hydroxide and carbon disulfide. The viscose is sprayed through fine holes into dilute sulfuric acid. This neutralizes the sodium hydroxide and turns the viscose into threads of rayon. Rayon is used for clothing, carpets, and bandages.

◀ *These cattle have no problem digesting cellulose, the tough carbohydrate molecule found in the cell walls of grass and other plants. People do not have the enzymes needed to digest cellulose, so it forms roughage, which helps food pass through the intestine properly.*

The Stuff of Life

Hydrogen atoms are found in some very complex molecules, such as deoxyribonucleic acid (DNA) and proteins. Many of them are involved in special chemical bonds, called hydrogen bonds.

What are hydrogen bonds?

Hydrogen bonds form between a hydrogen atom and an atom of fluorine, oxygen, or nitrogen. They can form between two molecules or parts of a large molecule. Hydrogen bonds are stronger than most other bonds between molecules. They increase the boiling points of small molecules and keep complex molecules in the correct shape.

Thank you, hydrogen bonds!

Molecules attracted to each other by weak bonds are easily separated by a little heat energy. As a result, they have low boiling points and are usually gases at room temperature. Hydrogen, oxygen, and nitrogen are all gases at room temperature because they are made from small molecules, but what about water?

Water, H_2O, is also a small molecule. It only contains three atoms and two of those are the smallest in the periodic table. This means that water ought to be a gas at room temperature, but it is a liquid instead. This is because hydrogen bonds form between water molecules and extra heat energy is needed to separate them. Without hydrogen bonds, the boiling point of water would be about −70 °C (−94 °F), not 100 °C (212 °F). The oceans, lakes, and rivers would all boil away, and life as we know it could not exist.

Get into shape with hydrogen bonds

DNA contains all the information a cell needs to function. A complex molecule, human DNA can be 7 centimeters (2.75 inches) long! Luckily, DNA is tightly rolled up to fit into the nuclei of cells. It is made from two long molecules or strands that twist around each other. They form a special spiral, called a double helix, that is held together by hydrogen bonds.

Proteins

Proteins are large molecules. There are many different types, which have a huge variety of jobs. Muscle, hair, and skin contain proteins. A protein called albumin is in egg white. Hydrogen bonds help to keep albumin molecules in shape. If egg white is cooked, the heat breaks the hydrogen bonds in the albumin and it becomes solid and white. Other proteins form natural catalysts called enzymes, such as those in yeast that convert sugar into ethanol. These are also sensitive to heat.

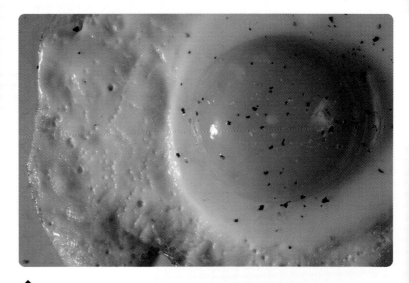

▲
Weak chemical bonds called hydrogen bonds help to keep proteins in their correct shapes. When an egg is cooked, the hydrogen bonds in its proteins are broken. This changes the egg white from a runny, almost see-through substance to a white solid.

Enzymes control the chemical reactions in cells, but they are damaged by changes in pH and temperatures above 45 °C (113 °F). Biological detergents contain enzymes to break down the fats in greasy stains. However, clothes have to be washed at low temperatures, otherwise the hydrogen bonds in the enzymes would break. Breaking the bonds changes the shape of the enzymes and stops them from working.

◀ *DNA is the complex molecule that controls the growth and development of all living things. In the model (opposite) of a small section of DNA, the hydrogen atoms are the white balls.*

Metal or Nonmetal?

Hydrogen is an unusual element in many ways. It is often placed alone in the periodic table and even when it is positioned above lithium in group 1, it does not really belong there. We usually think of hydrogen as a nonmetal, but it does have some properties of metals.

Properties of metals and nonmetals

The table gives a summary of some of the typical properties of metals and nonmetals.

Metals	Nonmetals
shiny	dull
high melting and boiling points	low melting and boiling points
high density (they feel heavy)	low density (they feel light)
strong	weak
malleable (bend without breaking)	brittle (break when bent or hit)
ductile (they make wires)	not ductile
good conductors of heat and electricity	good insulators
form positive ions in reactions	form negative ions in reactions
oxides are bases	oxides are acids

Hydrogen the metal

Hydrogen behaves like a metal whenever acids dissolve in water and form positively charged hydrogen ions, H^+. Scientists have also discovered that, like metals, hydrogen can be made to conduct electricity. Under extreme conditions of more than a million times atmospheric pressure, hydrogen turns into a liquid that conducts electricity. At even higher pressures, it turns into a solid that also conducts electricity.

Hydrogen the nonmetal

Hydrogen is a gas at room temperature and a good insulator. Just like a nonmetal, it reacts with other nonmetals to form molecules. We have seen many examples of these molecules in this book, such as ammonia, NH_3, and methane, CH_4. The really complicated molecules such as DNA, proteins, plastics, and sugars all contain hydrogen atoms joined to nonmetal atoms.

A little of both?

Metal oxides are bases and nonmetal oxides are acids when they are dissolved in water. But what about hydrogen? Water or hydrogen oxide, H_2O, is neutral.

Nonmetals such as chlorine and oxygen form negatively charged ions in reactions with metals. Chlorine forms chloride ions, Cl^-, and oxygen forms oxide ions, O^{2-}. Hydrogen forms hydride ions, H^-, when it reacts with reactive metals like lithium, making lithium hydride, LiH.

There are even more hydrides, such as lithium aluminum hydride, $LiAlH_4$, and sodium borohydride, $NaBH_4$. These are used as reducing agents by the chemical industry and can either remove oxygen atoms from molecules or add hydrogen atoms. They can change carboxylic acids back to alcohols, so acetic acid turns back into ethanol. They can also convert carboxylic acids into compounds called aldehydes. Methanal, HCHO, commonly known as formaldehyde, is an aldehyde used in sheep dips and as a preservative for biology specimens because it is a poisonous gas. Solutions of it will kill bacteria, insects, and fungi.

◀ *Formaldehyde is a rather smelly compound of carbon, hydrogen, and oxygen used to preserve biology specimens like this brain.*

CHAPTER 8

Here Comes the Sun

Hydrogen is the major element in the Sun and is a very flammable gas that burns easily in air. However, there is no air in space, so what is happening in the Sun? The answer to this question is that all the energy given off comes from nuclear reactions not chemical reactions.

Nuclear reactions

Chemical reactions happen when atoms swap or share electrons, but nuclear reactions occur when an atom's nucleus changes. The Sun uses a type of reaction called nuclear fusion. This occurs when the nuclei of two atoms crash into each other with so much energy that they stick together. The reaction forms the nucleus of a larger atom and releases lots of energy and radiation.

Fusion in the Sun

Fusion in the Sun happens in several stages, but generally four hydrogen-1 nuclei join together to make one helium-4 nucleus. The mass of a helium-4 nucleus is slightly less than the mass of four hydrogen-1 nuclei. Some of the leftover mass makes subatomic particles called neutrinos and positrons, but the rest is converted into energy.

Einstein's equation

Albert Einstein, a German physicist, discovered an equation that connects energy and mass. In his famous equation, $E=mc^2$, E stands for energy, m for mass, and c for the speed of light. As the speed of light is very fast (300,000,000 m/s [327,857,019 yds/s]), it means that a tiny mass can be converted into an enormous amount of energy.

Seven hundred million tons of hydrogen undergoes nuclear fusion in the Sun every second, producing nearly four billion billion megawatts of energy. On average, each square meter of Earth receives 1.36 kilowatts of energy from the Sun. The Sun provides light needed for plants to photosynthesize. It provides the heat that drives the water cycle, and it keeps Earth warm enough for life to exist.

Without the Sun, Earth would be frozen and lifeless. Plants such as this barley would not get the light they need to make their food. They would die and eventually people would all starve.

There goes the Sun

The Sun is a yellow dwarf star. It has been shining for nearly five billion years and has enough hydrogen for another five billion years. When the Sun begins to run out of hydrogen, gravity will make the Sun's core smaller, causing it to heat up. Eventually it will be hot enough to join helium nuclei together, making the nuclei of bigger atoms, such as carbon. Unfortunately, it will also make the outer layers of the Sun expand. They will expand so much, that the Sun will become a red giant, swallowing Earth and boiling it away.

(For more information on the Sun, see the table on page 62.)

The Sun is a gigantic nuclear fireball fueled by hydrogen. Its surface is constantly moving, and every so often huge solar flares erupt outwards and return to the surface. The one seen here is over 0.5 million kilometers (0.3 million miles) across.

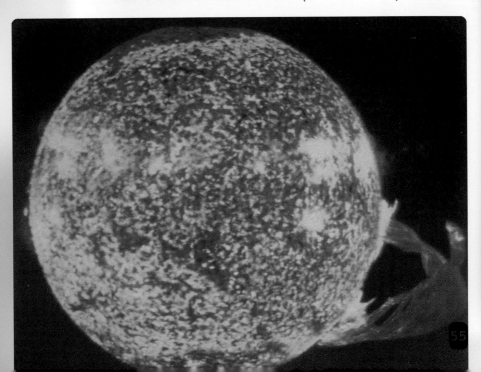

Copying Nature

The Sun uses hydrogen to produce immense amounts of energy by nuclear fusion. On Earth, the water molecules in the oceans contain enough hydrogen to power the Sun for seven years! Not suprisingly scientists are eager to copy what happens in the Sun. The first attempts at nuclear fusion on Earth were really very successful, except they made huge explosions rather than electricity.

Hydrogen bombs

Hydrogen bombs are incredibly powerful. Like the Sun, they work by making hydrogen nuclei join together. In 1952, the United States tested the first hydrogen bomb at Eniwetok Atoll in the Pacific Ocean. The bomb used liquid deuterium chilled by huge refrigeration equipment. Its devastating power destroyed an island and left a crater nearly 2 kilometers (1.24 miles) wide and 50 meters (55 yards) deep!

This fiery mushroom-shaped cloud was caused by the testing of a hydrogen bomb over Bikini Atoll in 1954. Hydrogen bombs are incredibly powerful. This explosion had the same power as eleven million tons of explosive. ▶

Deuterium and tritium on Earth

Harold Urey, an American scientist, discovered deuterium in 1931. Water containing deuterium (hydrogen-2) atoms, instead of ordinary hydrogen-1 atoms, is called heavy water. Tritium (hydrogen-3) is very rare on Earth. Cosmic rays from space cause it to form in the upper atmosphere, and it was first made artificially in 1934. Tritium is radioactive and was once used in luminous digital watch dials.

Modern hydrogen bombs work by forcing deuterium and tritium nuclei together. Liquid hydrogen is difficult to handle and tritium is rare and radioactive, so a solid called lithium deuteride is used instead. This is lithium hydride, LiH, made from deuterium instead of ordinary hydrogen-1.

An atomic bomb is used as a detonator, providing the energy and radiation needed to get the fusion reaction going. The radiation causes some of the lithium in the lithium deuteride to break apart to form tritium. In the tremendous heat and pressure caused by the detonator, nuclei join together and release huge amounts of energy. Tritium nuclei join with deuterium nuclei and deuterium nuclei also join together. The whole process takes about half a millionth of a second and would cause unimaginable disaster!

Atomic bombs

Atomic bombs use nuclear fission instead of nuclear fusion. This is when the nucleus of a large atom, such as uranium, breaks apart, forming nuclei of smaller atoms and releasing lots of energy and radiation. Little Boy, the first atomic bomb to be used in a war, was exploded on August 6, 1945, during World War II. It killed over 60,000 people in the Japanese city of Hiroshima.

Hot doughnuts

Attempts to use nuclear fusion to generate electricity have been less successful. Heating the mixture of deuterium and tritium to very high temperatures while keeping it inside the reactor is a major problem. Experimental reactors, called tokamaks, are shaped like hollow doughnuts. They use powerful magnetic fields to keep the hot mixture together and away from the walls. Research continues, but so far more energy is used than made. It may be years before all the problems are solved, but when they are, there will be an almost limitless supply of energy—until the Sun turns into a red dwarf.

Find out More about Hydrogen

The table below contains some information about the properties of hydrogen.

Element	Symbol	Atomic number	Melting point (°C)	Boiling point (°C)	State at 25 °C	Density at 25 °C (g/cm³)
hydrogen	H	1	−259	−253	gas	0.00115

The table below contains some information about the properties of hydrogen isotopes.

Isotope	Symbol	Mass number	Half-life	Radiation	Percent of natural hydrogen atoms
hydrogen-1 (protium)	$_1^1H$	1	stable	none	99.989
hydrogen-2 (deuterium)	$_1^2H$	2	stable	none	0.011
hydrogen-3 (tritium)	$_1^3H$	3	12.3 years	beta	0

Beta radiation, b, is caused by high-energy electrons shot out from the nucleus.

Compounds

These tables show you the chemical formulas of most of the compounds mentioned in this book. For example, ammonia has the formula NH_3. This means it is made from one nitrogen atom and three hydrogen atoms, joined together by chemical bonds.

Calcium compounds

Calcium compound	formula
calcium carbonate	$CaCO_3$
calcium chloride	$CaCl_2$
calcium hydrogen carbonate	$Ca(HCO_3)_2$
calcium oxide	CaO
calcium phosphate	$Ca_3(PO_4)_2$
calcium sulfate	$CaSO_4$

Carbon compound	formula
butane	C_4H_{10}
butanol	C_4H_9OH
carbon dioxide	CO_2
carbon disulfide	CS_2
ethane	C_2H_6
acetic acid	CH_3COOH
ethanol	C_2H_5OH
ethene	C_2H_4
glucose	$C_6H_{12}O_6$
methanal (formaldehyde)	$HCHO$
methane	CH_4
octanol	$C_8H_{17}OH$
octyl acetate	$CH_3COOC_8H_{17}$
pentanol	$C_5H_{11}OH$
pentyl acetate	$CH_3COOC_5H_{11}$
propane	C_3H_8
propene	C_3H_6

Carbon compounds

Lithium compound	formula
lithium aluminum hydride	$LiAlH_4$
lithium hydride	LiH

Lithium compounds

Nitrogen compound	formula
ammonia	NH_3
ammonium chloride	NH_4Cl
ammonium nitrate	NH_4NO_3
nitrogen monoxide	NO
nitroglycerine	$C_3H_5(ONO_2)_3$
trinitrotoluene	$CH_3C_6H_2(NO_2)_3$

Nitrogen compounds

Sodium compounds

Sodium compound	formula
sodium borohydride	$NaBH_4$
sodium carbonate	Na_2CO_3
sodium chloride	$NaCl$
sodium hydrogen carbonate	$NaHCO_3$
sodium hydroxide	$NaOH$
sodium tartrate	$Na_2C_4H_4O_6$

Sulphur compounds

Sulphur compound	formula
sulfur dioxide	SO_2
sulfur trioxide	SO_3

Other compounds

Compound	formula
aluminum oxide	Al_2O_3
cobalt chloride	$CoCl_2$
copper oxide	CuO
magnesium chloride	$MgCl_2$
potassium hydroxide	KOH
vanadium pentoxide	V_2O_5
hydrogen oxide (water)	H_2O
zinc sulfate	$ZnSO_4$

Acids

Acids	formula
carbonic acid	H_2CO_3
hydrochloric acid	HCl
nitric acid	HNO_3
phosphoric acid	H_3PO_4
sulfuric acid	H_2SO_4
tartaric acid	$H_2C_4H_4O_6$

Glossary

alloy mixture of two or more metals or mixture of a metal and a nonmetal

atom smallest particle of an element that has that element's properties

atomic number number of protons in the nucleus of an atom

bond force that join atoms together

catalyst substance that speeds up reactions without getting used up

compound substance made from the atoms of two or more elements, joined together by chemical bonds

density mass of a substance compared to its volume. Density equals mass divided by volume.

electron particle in an atom that has a negative electric charge. Electrons are found in shells around the nucleus of an atom.

element substance made from only one type of atom

enzyme substance made by living things that controls the chemical reactions that happen in the living thing

extract remove a chemical from a mixture of chemicals

fertilizer chemical that gives plants the elements they need for healthy growth

fossil fuel fuel that is formed from the ancient remains of plants and animals. Coal, oil, and natural gas are fossil fuels.

group vertical column of elements in the periodic table. Elements in a group have similar properties.

ion charged particle made when an atom loses or gains electrons

isotope atom of an element with the same number of protons and electrons, but different numbers of neutrons

mass number number of protons added to the number of neutrons in an atom's nucleus

molecule smallest particle of a compound that exists by itself. A molecule is made from two or more atoms joined together.

neutralize when an acid and an alkali or a base react together in a solution, thereby making it neutral, or neither acidic nor alkaline.

neutron particle in an atom's nucleus that does not have an electric charge

nuclear reaction reaction involving the nucleus of an atom

nucleus central part of an atom made from protons and neutrons. It has a positive electric charge.

period horizontal row of elements in the periodic table

periodic table table in which all the known elements are arranged into groups and periods

product substance made in a chemical reaction

proton particle in an atom's nucleus that has a positive electric charge

radiation energy or particles given off when an atom decays or breaks down

radioactive producing radiation

reaction chemical change that produces new substances

salt chemical formed when an acid is neutralized

spectrum all the different colors that make up a ray of light

subatomic particle particle smaller than an atom, such as a proton, neutron, and electron

welding joining two or more metals together, usually by heating them

Sun Facts

The Sun contains huge amounts of hydrogen. This table contains some information about the Sun.

	Actual amount	A comparison to help
distance from Earth	149,600,000 km (92,957,000 mi.)	London to New York (and back) 13,000 times
diameter of the Sun	1,390,000 km (863,706 mi.)	London to New York (and back) 124 times
mass of the Sun	1.989 octillion kilograms	330,000 times the mass of the earth
surface temperature	5.530 °C (9,986 °F)	three times the melting point of iron
inside temperature	15,600,000 °C (28,080,032 °F)	8,600 times the melting point of iron
energy output	383 billion trillion kilowatts	equal to 100 billion tons of TNT exploding each second
mass of hydrogen fuel used	7,000,000,000 tons per second	extracting and using the hydrogen from a ball of water 2 km (1.24 mi.) in diameter every second

Timeline

discovers a flammable gas and calls it inflammable air	1766	Henry Cavendish
names it hydrogen; discovers that hydrogen burns in air to produce water	1783	Antoine Lavoisier
discovers hydrogen in the Sun by studying the spectrum of sunlight	1862	Anders Ångström
deuterium discovered	1931	Harold Urey
tritium discovered	1934	Lord Rutherford
invention of the gas battery, the first hydrogen fuel cell	1842	William Grove
test detonation of the world's first hydrogen bomb in the Pacific Ocean	1952	United States

Further Reading and Useful Websites

Books

Bankston, John. *Edward Teller and the Development of the Hydrogen Bomb.* Hockessin, Del.: Mitchell Lane Publishers, Inc., 2001.

Oxlade, Chris. *Acids and Bases.* Chicago: Heinemann Library, 2002.

Oxlade, Chris. *Elements and Compounds.* Chicago: Heinemann Library, 2002.

Websites

WebElements™
http://www.webelements.com
An interactive periodic table crammed with information and photographs.

DiscoverySchool
http://school.discovery.comclipart
Help for science projects and homework. Free science clip art is available.

Proton Don
http://www.funbrain.com/periodic
The fun periodic table quiz!

Index